CHRISTIAN
MARRIAGE

Encyclical Letter

CHRISTIAN MARRIAGE

OF HIS HOLINESS POPE PIUS XI

BOOKS & MEDIA

BOSTON

ISBN 0-8198-1488-1

Vatican Translation

Printed and published in the U.S.A. by Pauline Books & Media, 50 Saint Pauls Avenue, Boston MA 02130-3491.

www.pauline.org

Pauline Books & Media is the publishing house of the Daughters of St. Paul, an international congregation of women religious serving the Church with the communications media.

1 2 3 4 5 6   06 05 04 03 02 01

CONTENTS

*To Our Venerable Brethren, Patriarchs,
Primates, Archbishops, Bishops and
other Local Ordinaries enjoying peace
and communion with the Apostolic See.
Venerable Brethren and Beloved Children,
Health and Apostolic Benediction.*

1. How great is the dignity of chaste wedlock, Venerable Brethren, may be judged best from this that Christ Our Lord, Son of the Eternal Father, having assumed the nature of fallen man, not only, with his loving desire of compassing the redemption of our race, ordained it in a special manner as the principle and foundation of domestic society and therefore of all human intercourse, but also raised it to the rank of a truly great sacrament of the New Law, restored it to the original purity of its divine institution, and accordingly entrusted all its discipline and care to his spouse the Church.

2. In order, however, that among men of every nation and every age the desired fruits may be obtained from this renewal of matrimony, it is necessary, first of all, that men's minds be illuminated with the true doctrine of Christ regarding it; and second, that Christian spouses, the weakness of their wills strengthened by the internal grace of God, shape all their ways of thinking and of acting in conformity with that pure law of Christ so as to obtain true peace and happiness for themselves and for their families.

3. Yet not only do We, looking with paternal eye on the universal world from this Apostolic See as from a watchtower, but you, also, Venerable Brethren, see, and seeing deeply grieve with Us that a great number of men, forgetful of that divine work of redemption, either entirely ignore or shamelessly deny the great sanctity of Christian wedlock, or relying on the false principles of a new and utterly perverse morality, too often trample it underfoot. And since these most pernicious errors and depraved morals have begun to spread even among the faithful and are gradually gaining ground, in Our office as Christ's Vicar upon earth and Supreme Shepherd and Teacher, We consider it Our duty to raise Our voice to keep the flock committed to Our care from poisoned pastures and, as far as in Us lies, to preserve it from harm.

4. We have decided, therefore, to speak to you, Venerable Brethren, and through you to the whole Church of Christ and indeed to the whole human race, on the nature and dignity of Christian marriage, on the advantages and benefits which accrue from it to the family and to human society itself, on the errors contrary to this most important point of the Gospel teaching, on the vices opposed to conjugal union, and lastly on the principal remedies to be applied. In so doing We follow the footsteps of Our predecessor, Leo XIII, of happy memory, whose Encyclical *Arcanum,*[1] published fifty years ago, We hereby confirm and make Our own, and while We wish to expound more fully certain points called for by the circumstances of our times, nevertheless We declare that, far from being obsolete, it retains its full force at the present day.

---

1. Encyclical *Arcanum Divinae Sapientiae,* Feb. 10, 1880.

I.

NATURE AND DIGNITY
OF CHRISTIAN MARRIAGE

5. And to begin with that same encyclical, which is wholly concerned in vindicating the divine institution of matrimony, its sacramental dignity, and its perpetual stability, let it be repeated as an immutable and inviolable fundamental doctrine that matrimony was not instituted or restored by man but by God; not by man were the laws made to strengthen and confirm and elevate it but by God, the Author of nature, and by Christ Our Lord by whom nature was redeemed, and hence these laws cannot be subject to any human decrees or to any contrary pact even of the spouses themselves. This is the doctrine of Holy Scripture;[2] this is the constant tradition of the Universal Church; this the solemn definition of the sacred Council of Trent, which declares and establishes from the words of Holy Writ itself that God is the Author of the perpetual stability of the marriage bond, its unity and its firmness.[3]

6. Yet although matrimony is of its very nature of divine institution, the human will, too, enters into it and performs a most noble part. For each individual marriage, inasmuch as it

---

2. Gen 1:27–28; 2:22–23; Mt 19:3ff.; Eph 5:33ff.
3. Council of Trent, Sess. 24.

is a conjugal union of a particular man and woman, arises only from the free consent of each of the spouses; and this free act of the will, by which each party hands over and accepts those rights proper to the state of marriage,[4] is so necessary to constitute true marriage that it cannot be supplied by any human power.[5] This freedom, however, regards only the question whether the contracting parties really wish to enter upon matrimony or to marry this particular person; but the nature of matrimony is entirely independent of the free will of man, so that if one has once contracted matrimony he is thereby subject to its divinely made laws and its essential properties. For the Angelic Doctor, writing on conjugal honor and on the offspring which is the fruit of marriage, says: "These things are so contained in matrimony by the marriage pact itself that, if anything to the contrary were expressed in the consent which makes the marriage, it would not be a true marriage."[6]

7. By matrimony, therefore, the souls of the contracting parties are joined and knit together more directly and more intimately than are their bodies, and that not by any passing affection of sense of spirit, but by a deliberate and firm act of the will; and from this union of souls by God's decree, a sacred and inviolable bond arises. Hence the nature of this contract, which is proper and peculiar to it alone, makes it entirely different both from the union of animals entered into by the blind instinct of nature alone in which neither reason nor free will plays a part, and also from the haphazard unions

---

4. *Code of Canon Law,* can. 1081 § 2.*

5. *Code of Canon Law,* can. 1081 § 1.

6. St. Thomas Aquinas, *Summa Theol.,* III, Supplem. 9, 49, art. 3.

of men, which are far removed from all true and honorable unions of will and enjoy none of the rights of family life.

8. From this it is clear that legitimately constituted authority has the right and therefore the duty to restrict, to prevent, and to punish those base unions which are opposed to reason and to nature; but since it is a matter which flows from human nature itself, no less certain is the teaching of Our predecessor, Leo XIII of happy memory:[7] "In choosing a state of life there is no doubt but that it is in the power and discretion of each one to prefer one or the other: either to embrace the counsel of virginity given by Jesus Christ, or to bind himself in the bonds of matrimony. To take away from man the natural and primeval right of marriage, to circumscribe in any way the principal ends of marriage laid down in the beginning by God himself in the words 'increase and multiply' (Gen 1:28), is beyond the power of any human law."

9. Therefore the sacred partnership of true marriage is constituted both by the will of God and the will of man. From God comes the very institution of marriage, the ends for which it was instituted, the laws that govern it, the blessings that flow from it; while man, through generous surrender of his own person made to another for the whole span of life, becomes, with the help and cooperation of God, the author of each particular marriage, with the duties and blessings annexed thereto from divine institution.

---

7. Encyclical *Rerum Novarum,* May 15, 1891.

* The footnote references to canon law found in this document refer to the 1917 code, which was in effect at the time this encyclical was written. Current Church laws concerning marriage are found in the new *Code of Canon Law* first published in 1983 (see canons 1055–1165 and 1671–1707).

II.

BLESSINGS AND BENEFITS OF MATRIMONY

10. Now when We come to explain, Venerable Brethren, what are the blessings that God has attached to true matrimony, and how great they are, there occur to Us the words of that illustrious Doctor of the Church whom We commemorated recently in Our Encyclical *Ad Salute* on the occasion of the fifteenth centenary of his death:[8] "These," says St. Augustine, "are all the blessings of matrimony on account of which matrimony itself is a blessing; offspring, conjugal faith and the sacrament."[9] And how under these three heads is contained a splendid summary of the whole doctrine of Christian marriage, the holy Doctor himself expressly declares when he says: "By conjugal faith it is provided that there should be no carnal intercourse outside the marriage bond with another man or woman; with regard to offspring, that children should be begotten of love, tenderly cared for and educated in a religious atmosphere; finally, in its sacramental aspect, that the marriage bond should not be broken and that a husband or wife, if separated, should not be joined to another even for the sake of offspring. This we regard as the law of marriage by

---

8. Encyclical *Ad Salutem,* April 20, 1930.
9. St. Augustine, *De bono coniug.,* cap. 24, n. 32.

which the fruitfulness of nature is adorned and the evil of incontinence is restrained."[10]

11. Thus among the blessings of marriage, the child holds the first place. And indeed the Creator of the human race himself, Who in his goodness wishes to use men as his helpers in the propagation of life, taught this when, instituting marriage in Paradise, he said to our first parents, and through them to all future spouses: "Increase and multiply, and fill the earth" (Gen 1:28). As St. Augustine admirably deduces from the words of the holy Apostle St. Paul to Timothy (1 Tim 5:14) when he says: "The Apostle himself is therefore a witness that marriage is for the sake of generation: 'I wish,' he says, 'young girls to marry.' And, as if someone said to him, 'Why?' he immediately adds: 'To bear children, to be mothers of families.'"[11]

12. How great a boon of God this is, and how great a blessing of matrimony is clear from a consideration of man's dignity and of his sublime end. For man surpasses all other visible creatures by the superiority of his rational nature alone. Besides, God wishes men to be born not only that they should live and fill the earth, but much more that they may be worshippers of God, that they may know him and love him and finally enjoy him forever in heaven; and this end, since man is raised by God in a marvelous way to the supernatural order, surpasses all that eye has seen, and ear heard, and all that has entered into the heart of man (1 Cor 2:9). From which it is easily seen how great a gift of divine goodness and how

---

10. St. Augustine, *De Gen. ad litt.,* lib. IX, cap. 7, n. 12.

11. St. Augustine, *De bono coniug.,* cap. 24, n. 32.

remarkable a fruit of marriage are children born by the omnipotent power of God through the cooperation of those bound in wedlock.

13. But Christian parents must also understand that they are destined not only to propagate and preserve the human race on earth, indeed not only to educate any kind of worshippers of the true God, but children who are to become members of the Church of Christ, to raise up fellow citizens of the saints, and members of God's household (Eph 2:19), that the worshippers of God and Our Savior may daily increase.

14. For although Christian spouses even if sanctified themselves cannot transmit sanctification to their progeny, nay, although the very natural process of generating life has become the way of death by which original sin is passed on to posterity, nevertheless, they share to some extent in the blessings of that primeval marriage of Paradise, since it is theirs to offer their offspring to the Church in order that by this most fruitful Mother of the children of God they may be regenerated through the laver of Baptism unto supernatural justice and finally be made living members of Christ, partakers of immortal life, and heirs of that eternal glory to which we all aspire from our inmost heart.

15. If a true Christian mother weigh well these things, she will indeed understand with a sense of deep consolation that of her the words of Our Savior were spoken: "A woman... when she has brought forth the child remembers no more the anguish, for joy that a man is born into the world" (Jn 16:21); and proving herself superior to all the pains and cares and solicitudes of her maternal office with a more just and holy joy than that of the Roman matron, the mother of the

Gracchi, she will rejoice in the Lord crowned as it were with the glory of her offspring. Both husband and wife, however, receiving these children with joy and gratitude from the hand of God, will regard them as a talent committed to their charge by God, not only to be employed for their own advantage or for that of an earthly commonwealth, but to be restored to God with interest on the day of reckoning.

Education of Children Is the Parents' Duty

16. The blessing of offspring, however, is not completed by the mere begetting of them, but something else must be added, namely the proper education of the offspring. For the most wise God would have failed to make sufficient provision for children that had been born, and so for the whole human race, if he had not given to those to whom he had entrusted the power and right to beget them, the power also and the right to educate them. For no one can fail to see that children are incapable of providing wholly for themselves, even in matters pertaining to their natural life, and much less in those pertaining to the supernatural, but require for many years to be helped, instructed and educated by others. Now it is certain that both by the law of nature and of God this right and duty of educating their offspring belongs in the first place to those who began the work of nature by giving them birth, and they are indeed forbidden to leave unfinished this work and so expose it to certain ruin. But in matrimony provision has been made in the best possible way for this education of children that is so necessary, for, since the parents are bound together

by an indissoluble bond, the care and mutual help of each is always at hand.

17. Since, however, We have spoken fully elsewhere on the Christian education of youth,[12] let Us sum it all up by quoting once more the words of St. Augustine: "As regards the offspring it is provided that they should be begotten lovingly and educated religiously"[13]—and this is also expressed succinctly in the *Code of Canon Law*—"The primary end of marriage is the procreation and the education of children."[14]

18. Nor must We omit to remark, in fine, that since the duty entrusted to parents for the good of their children is of such high dignity and of such great importance, every use of the faculty given by God for the procreation of new life is the right and the privilege of the married state alone, by the law of God and of nature, and must be confined absolutely within the sacred limits of that state.

Conjugal Fidelity

19. The second blessing of matrimony which We said was mentioned by St. Augustine, is the blessing of conjugal honor which consists in the mutual fidelity of the spouses in fulfilling the marriage contract, so that what belongs to one of the parties by reason of this contract sanctioned by divine law, may not be denied to him or permitted to any third person; nor

---

12. Encyclical *Divini Illius Magistri,* Dec. 31, 1929.

13. St. Augustine, *De Gen. ad litt.,* lib. IX, cap. 7, n. 12.

14. *Code of Canon Law,* can. 1013 § 7.

may there be conceded to one of the parties anything which, being contrary to the rights and laws of God and entirely opposed to matrimonial faith, can never be conceded.

20. Wherefore, conjugal faith, or honor, demands in the first place the complete unity of matrimony which the Creator himself laid down in the beginning when he wished it to be not otherwise than between one man and one woman. And although afterward this primeval law was relaxed to some extent by God, the Supreme Legislator, there is no doubt that the law of the Gospel fully restored that original and perfect unity, and abrogated all dispensations as the words of Christ and the constant teaching and action of the Church show plainly. With reason, therefore, does the Sacred Council of Trent solemnly declare: "Christ Our Lord very clearly taught that in this bond two persons only are to be united and joined together when he said: 'Therefore they are no longer two, but one flesh.'"[15]

21. Nor did Christ Our Lord wish only to condemn any form of polygamy or polyandry, as they are called, whether successive or simultaneous, and every other external dishonorable act, but, in order that the sacred bonds of marriage may be guarded absolutely inviolate, he forbade also even willful thoughts and desires of such like things: "But I say to you, that whosoever shall look on a woman to lust after her has already committed adultery with her in his heart" (Mt 5:28). These words of Christ Our Lord cannot be annulled even by the consent of one of the partners of marriage, for they ex-

---

15. Council of Trent, Sess. 24.

press a law of God and of nature which no will of man can break or bend.[16]

22. Nay, that mutual familiar intercourse between the spouses themselves, if the blessing of conjugal faith is to shine with becoming splendor, must be distinguished by chastity so that husband and wife bear themselves in all things with the law of God and of nature, and endeavor always to follow the will of their most wise and holy Creator with the greatest reverence toward the work of God.

Love of Husband and Wife

23. This conjugal faith, however, which is most aptly called by St. Augustine the "faith of chastity" blooms more freely, more beautifully and more nobly when it is rooted in that more excellent soil, the love of husband and wife which pervades all the duties of married life and holds pride of place in Christian marriage. For matrimonial faith demands that husband and wife be joined in an especially holy and pure love, not as adulterers love each other, but as Christ loved the Church. This precept the Apostle laid down when he said: "Husbands, love your wives as Christ also loved the Church" (Eph 5:25; Col 3:19), that Church which of a truth he embraced with a boundless love not for the sake of his own advantage, but seeking only the good of his Spouse.[17] The love, then, of which We are speaking is not that based on the passing lust of the moment nor does it consist in pleasing

16. Decree of the Holy Office, March 2, 1679, propos. 50.
17. *Roman Catechism,* II, cap. 8, q. 24.

words only, but in the deep attachment of the heart which is expressed in action, since love is proved by deeds.[18] This outward expression of love in the home demands not only mutual help but must go further; it must have as its primary purpose that man and wife help each other day by day in forming and perfecting themselves in the interior life, so that through their partnership in life they may advance ever more and more in virtue, and above all that they may grow in true love toward God and their neighbor, on which indeed "depends the whole Law and the Prophets" (Mt 22:40). For all men of every condition, in whatever honorable walk of life they may be, can and ought to imitate that most perfect example of holiness placed before man by God, namely Christ Our Lord, and by God's grace arrive at the summit of perfection, as is proved by the example set us by many saints.

24. This mutual molding of husband and wife, this determined effort to perfect each other, can in a very real sense, as the *Roman Catechism* teaches, be said to be the chief reason and purpose of matrimony, provided matrimony be looked at not in the restricted sense as instituted for the proper conception and education of the child, but more widely as the blending of life as a whole and the mutual interchange and sharing thereof.

25. By this same love it is necessary that all the other rights and duties of the marriage state be regulated by the words of the Apostle: "Let the husband render the debt to the

---

18. St. Gregory the Great, *Homil. XXX in Evang.* (Jn 14:23–31), n.1.

wife, and the wife also in like manner to the husband" (1 Cor 7:3), which express not only a law of justice but of charity.

26. Domestic society being confirmed, therefore, by this bond of love, there should flourish in it that "order of love," as St. Augustine calls it. This order includes both the primacy of the husband with regard to the wife and children, the ready subjection of the wife and her willing obedience, which the Apostle commends in these words: "Let women be subject to their husbands as to the Lord, because the husband is the head of the wife, and Christ is the head of the Church" (Eph 5: 22–23).

27. This subjection, however, does not deny or take away the liberty which fully belongs to the woman both in view of her dignity as a human person, and in view of her most noble office as wife and mother and companion; nor does it bid her obey her husband's every request if not in harmony with right reason or with the dignity due to wife; nor, in fine, does it imply that the wife should be put on a level with those persons who in law are called minors, to whom it is not customary to allow free exercise of their rights on account of their lack of mature judgment, or of their ignorance of human affairs. But it forbids that exaggerated liberty which cares not for the good of the family; it forbids that in this body which is the family, the heart be separated from the head to the great detriment of the whole body and the proximate danger of ruin. For if the man is the head, the woman is the heart, and as he occupies the chief place in ruling, so she may and ought to claim for herself the chief place in love.

28. Again, this subjection of wife to husband in its degree and manner may vary according to the different conditions of

persons, place and time. In fact, if the husband neglect his duty, it falls to the wife to take his place in directing the family. But the structure of the family and its fundamental law, established and confirmed by God, must always and everywhere be maintained intact.

29. With great wisdom Our predecessor Leo XIII, of happy memory, in the encyclical on Christian marriage which We have already mentioned, speaking of this order to be maintained between man and wife, teaches: "The man is the ruler of the family, and the head of the woman; but because she is flesh of his flesh and bone of his bone, let her be subject and obedient to the man, not as a servant but as a companion, so that nothing be lacking of honor or of dignity in the obedience which she pays. Let divine charity be the constant guide of their mutual relations, both in him who rules and in her who obeys, since each bears the image, the one of Christ, the other of the Church."[19]

30. These, then, are the elements which compose the blessing of conjugal faith: unity, chastity, charity, honorable and noble obedience, which are at the same time an enumeration of the benefits which are bestowed on husband and wife in their married state, benefits by which the peace, the dignity and the happiness of matrimony are securely preserved and fostered. Wherefore it is not surprising that this conjugal faith has always been counted among the most priceless and special blessings of matrimony.

---

19. Encyclical *Arcanum Divinae Sapientiae,* Feb. 10, 1880.

Indissolubility

31. But this accumulation of benefits is completed and, as it were, crowned by that blessing of Christian marriage which, in the words of St. Augustine, we have called the sacrament, by which is denoted both the indissolubility of the bond and the raising and hallowing of the contract by Christ himself, whereby he made it an efficacious sign of grace.

32. In the first place Christ himself lays stress on the indissolubility and firmness of the marriage bond when he says: "What God has joined together let no man put asunder" (Mt 19:6), and "Everyone who puts away his wife and marries another commits adultery, and he who marries her who is put away from her husband commits adultery" (Lk 16:18).

33. And St. Augustine clearly places what he calls the blessing of matrimony in this indissolubility when he says: "In the sacrament it is provided that the marriage bond should not be broken, and that a husband or wife, if separated, should not be joined to another even for the sake of offspring."[20]

34. And this inviolable stability, although not in the same perfect measure in every case, belongs to every true marriage, for the word of the Lord—"What God has joined together let no man put asunder"—must of necessity include all true marriages without exception, since it was spoken of the marriage of our first parents, the prototype of every future marriage. Therefore, although before Christ the sublimeness and the severity of the primeval law was so tempered that Moses permitted to the chosen people of God on account of the

---

20. St. Augustine, *De Gen. ad litt.,* lib. IX, cap. 7, n. 12.

hardness of their hearts that a bill of divorce might be given in certain circumstances, nevertheless, Christ, by virtue of his supreme legislative power, recalled this concession of greater liberty and restored the primeval law in its integrity by those words which must never be forgotten, "What God hath joined together let no man put asunder." Wherefore, Our predecessor Pius VI of happy memory, writing to the Bishop of Aria, most wisely said: "Hence it is clear that marriage even in the state of nature, and certainly long before it was raised to the dignity of a sacrament, was divinely instituted in such a way that it should carry with it a perpetual and indissoluble bond which cannot therefore be dissolved by any civil law. Therefore, although the sacramental element may be absent from a marriage as is the case among unbelievers, still in such a marriage, inasmuch as it is a true marriage, there must remain and indeed there does remain that perpetual bond which by divine right is so bound up with matrimony from its first institution that it is not subject to any civil power. And so, whatever marriage is said to be contracted, either it is so contracted that it is really a true marriage, in which case it carries with it that enduring bond which by divine right is inherent in every true marriage; or it is thought to be contracted without that perpetual bond, and in that case there is no marriage, but an illicit union opposed of its very nature to the divine law, which therefore cannot be entered into or maintained."[21]

35. And if this stability seems to be open to exception, however rare the exception may be, as in the case of certain natural marriages between unbelievers, or among Christians

---

21. Pius VI, *Rescript. ad Episc. Agriens.,* July 11, 1789.

in the case of those marriages which though valid have not been consummated, that exception does not depend on the will of men nor on that of any merely human power, but on divine law, of which the only guardian and interpreter is the Church of Christ. However, not even this power can ever affect for any cause whatsoever a Christian marriage which is valid and has been consummated, for as it is plain that here the marriage contract has its full completion, so, by the will of God, there is also the greatest firmness and indissolubility which may not be destroyed by any human authority.

36. If we wish with all reverence to inquire into the intimate reason of this divine decree, Venerable Brethren, we shall easily see it in the mystical signification of Christian marriage, which is fully and perfectly verified in consummated marriage between Christians. For, as the Apostle says in his Epistle to the Ephesians (5:32), the marriage of Christians recalls that most perfect union which exists between Christ and the Church: *"Sacramento hoc magnum est, ego autem deco, in Christo et in ecclesia;"* which union, as long as Christ shall live and the Church through him, can never be dissolved by any separation. And this St. Augustine clearly declares in these words: "This is safeguarded in Christ and the Church, which, living with Christ who lives forever, may never be divorced from him. The observance of this sacrament is such in the City of God...that is, in the Church of Christ, that when for the sake of begetting children, women marry or are taken to wife, it is wrong to leave a wife that is sterile in order to take another by whom children may be had. Anyone doing this is guilty of adultery, just as if he married another, guilty not by the law of the day, according to which

when one's partner is put away another may be taken, which the Lord allowed in the law of Moses because of the hardness of the hearts of the people of Israel, but by the law of the Gospel."[22]

Benefits of Indissolubility

37. Indeed, how many and how important are the benefits which flow from the indissolubility of matrimony cannot escape anyone who gives even a brief consideration either to the good of the married parties and the offspring or to the welfare of human society. First of all, both husband and wife possess a positive guarantee of the endurance of this stability, which that generous yielding of their persons and the intimate fellowship of their hearts by their nature strongly require, since true love never falls away (1 Cor 13:8). Besides, a strong bulwark is set up in defense of a loyal chastity against incitements to infidelity, should any be encountered either from within or from without; any anxious fear lest in adversity or old age the other spouse would prove unfaithful is precluded, and in its place there reigns a calm sense of security. Moreover, the dignity of both man and wife is maintained and mutual aid is most satisfactorily assured, while through the indissoluble bond, always enduring, the spouses are warned continuously that not for the sake of perishable things nor that they may serve their passions, but that they may procure one for the other high and lasting good, have they entered into the nuptial partnership, to be dissolved only by death. In the

---

22. St. Augustine, *De nupt. et concup.,* lib. 1, cap. 10.

training and education of children, which must extend over a period of many years, it plays a great part, since the grave and long enduring burdens of this office are best borne by the united efforts of the parents. Nor do lesser benefits accrue to human society as a whole. For experience has taught that unassailable stability in matrimony is a fruitful source of virtuous life and of habits of integrity. Where this order of things obtains, the happiness and well-being of the nation is safely guarded; what the families and individuals are, so also is the State, for a body is determined by its parts. Wherefore, both for the private good of husband, wife and children, as likewise for the public good of human society, they indeed deserve well who strenuously defend the inviolable stability of matrimony.

Sacramental Graces

38. But considering the benefits of the sacrament, besides the firmness and indissolubility, there are also much higher emoluments as the word "sacrament" itself very aptly indicates; for to Christians this is not a meaningless and empty name. Christ the Lord, the Institutor and "Perfecter" of the holy sacraments,[23] by raising the matrimony of his faithful to the dignity of a true sacrament of the New Law, made it a sign and source of that peculiar internal grace by which "it perfects natural love, it confirms an indissoluble union, and sanctifies both man and wife."[24]

---

23. Council of Trent, Sess. 24.
24. Council of Trent, Sess. 24.

39. And since the valid matrimonial consent among the faithful was constituted by Christ as a sign of grace, the sacramental nature is so intimately bound up with Christian wedlock that there can be no true marriage between baptized persons "without it being by that very fact a sacrament."[25]

40. By the very fact, therefore, that the faithful with sincere mind give such consent, they open up for themselves a treasure of sacramental grace from which they draw supernatural power for the fulfilling of their rights and duties faithfully, holily, perseveringly even unto death. Hence this sacrament not only increases sanctifying grace, the permanent principle of the supernatural life, in those who, as the expression is, place no obstacle *(obex)* in its way, but also adds particular gifts, dispositions and seeds of grace, by elevating and perfecting the natural powers. By these gifts the parties are assisted not only in understanding, but in knowing intimately, in adhering to firmly, in willing effectively, and in successfully putting into practice those things which pertain to the marriage state, its aims and duties, giving them in fine right to the actual assistance of grace, whensoever they need it for fulfilling the duties of their state.

41. Nevertheless, since it is a law of divine Providence in the supernatural order that men do not reap the full fruit of the sacraments which they receive after acquiring the use of reason unless they cooperate with grace, the grace of matrimony will remain for the most part an unused talent hidden in the field unless the parties exercise these supernatural powers and cultivate and develop the seeds of grace they have received.

---

25. *Code of Canon Law,* can. 1012.

If, however, doing all that lies with their power, they cooperate diligently, they will be able with ease to bear the burdens of their state and to fulfill their duties. By such a sacrament they will be strengthened, sanctified and in a manner consecrated. For, as St. Augustine teaches, just as by Baptism and Holy Orders a man is set aside and assisted either for the duties of Christian life or for the priestly office and is never deprived of their sacramental aid, almost in the same way (although not by a sacramental character), the faithful once joined by marriage ties can never be deprived of the help and the binding force of the sacrament. Indeed, as the Holy Doctor adds, even those who commit adultery carry with them that sacred yoke, although in this case not as a title to the glory of grace but for the ignominy of their guilty action, "as the soul by apostasy, withdrawing as it were from marriage with Christ, even though it may have lost its faith, does not lose the sacrament of Faith which it received at the laver of regeneration."[26]

42. These parties, let it be noted, not fettered but adorned by the golden bond of the sacrament, not hampered but assisted, should strive with all their might to the end that their wedlock, not only through the power and symbolism of the sacrament, but also through their spirit and manner of life, may be and remain always the living image of that most fruitful union of Christ with the Church, which is to be venerated as the sacred token of most perfect love.

43. All of these things, Venerable Brethren, you must consider carefully and ponder over with a lively faith if you

---

26. St. Augustine, *De nupt. et concup.,* lib. I, cap. 10.

would see in their true light the extraordinary benefits of matrimony—offspring, conjugal faith and the sacrament. No one can fail to admire the divine Wisdom, Holiness and Goodness which, while respecting the dignity and happiness of husband and wife, has provided so bountifully for the conservation and propagation of the human race by a single chaste and sacred fellowship of nuptial union.

III.

FALSE THEORIES

44. When we consider the great excellence of chaste wedlock, Venerable Brethren, it appears all the more regrettable that particularly in our day we should witness this divine institution often scorned and on every side degraded.

45. For now, alas, not secretly nor under cover, but openly, with all sense of shame put aside, now by word, again by writings, by theatrical productions of every kind, by romantic fiction, by amorous and frivolous novels, by cinematographs portraying in vivid scene, in addresses broadcast by radio telephony, in short by all the inventions of modern science, the sanctity of marriage is trampled upon and derided; divorce, adultery and all the basest vices either are extolled or at least are depicted in such colors as to appear to be free of all reproach and infamy. Books are not lacking which dare to pronounce themselves as scientific, but which in truth are merely coated with a veneer of science in order that they may the more easily insinuate their ideas. The doctrines defended in these are offered for sale as the productions of modern genius, of that genius namely, which, anxious only for truth, is considered to have *emancipated* itself from all those old-fashioned and immature opinions of the ancients; and to the number of these antiquated opinions they relegate the traditional doctrine of Christian marriage.

46. These thoughts are instilled into men of every class, rich and poor, masters and workers, lettered and unlettered, married and single, the godly and godless, old and young, but for these last, as easiest prey, the worst snares are laid.

47. Not all the sponsors of these new doctrines are carried to the extremes of unbridled lust; there are those who, striving as it were to ride a middle course, believe nevertheless that something should be conceded in our times as regards certain precepts of the divine and natural law. But these likewise, more or less wittingly, are emissaries of the great enemy who is ever seeking to sow cockle among the wheat (Mt 13:25). We, therefore, whom the Father has appointed over his field, We who are bound by Our most holy office to take care lest the good seed be choked by the weeds, believe it fitting to apply to Ourselves the most grave words of the Holy Ghost with which the Apostle Paul exhorted his beloved Timothy: "Be vigilant.... Fulfill your ministry.... Preach the word, be persistent in season, out of season, reprove, entreat, rebuke in all patience and doctrine" (2 Tim 4:2–5).

48. And since, in order that the deceits of the enemy may be avoided, it is necessary first of all that they be laid bare; since much is to be gained by denouncing these fallacies for the sake of the unwary, even though We prefer not to name these iniquities "as becomes saints" (Eph 5:3), yet for the welfare of souls We cannot remain altogether silent.

Denial of Divine Institution

49. To begin at the very source of these evils, their basic principle lies in this, that matrimony is repeatedly declared to

be not instituted by the Author of nature nor raised by Christ the Lord to the dignity of a true sacrament, but invented by man. Some confidently assert that they have found no evidence of the existence of matrimony in nature or in her laws, but regard it merely as the means of producing life and of gratifying in one way or another a vehement impulse; on the other hand, others recognize that certain beginnings or, as it were, seeds of true wedlock are found in the nature of man since, unless men were bound together by some form of permanent tie, the dignity of husband and wife or the natural end of propagating and rearing the offspring would not receive satisfactory provision. At the same time they maintain that in all beyond this germinal idea matrimony, through various concurrent causes, is invented solely by the mind of man, established solely by his will.

50. How grievously all these err and how shamelessly they leave the ways of honesty is already evident from what we have set forth here regarding the origin and nature of wedlock, its purposes and the good inherent in it. The evil of this teaching is plainly seen from the consequences which its advocates deduce from it, namely, that the laws, institutions and customs by which wedlock is governed, since they take their origin solely from the will of man, are subject entirely to him, hence can and must be founded, changed and abrogated according to human caprice and the shifting circumstances of human affairs; that the generative power which is grounded in nature itself is more sacred and has wider range than matrimony—hence it may be exercised both outside as well as within the confines of wedlock, and though the purpose of matrimony be set aside, as though to suggest that the license

of a base fornicating woman should enjoy the same rights as the chaste motherhood of a lawfully wedded wife.

51. Armed with these principles, some men go so far as to concoct new species of unions, suited, as they say, to the present temper of men and the times, which various new forms of matrimony they presume to label "temporary," "experimental" and "companionate." These offer all the indulgence of matrimony and its rights without, however, the indissoluble bond, and without offspring, unless later the parties alter their cohabitation into a matrimony in the full sense of the law.

52. Indeed there are some who desire and insist that these practices be legitimatized by the law or, at least, excused by their general acceptance among the people. They do not seem even to suspect that these proposals partake of nothing of the modern "culture" in which they glory so much, but are simply hateful abominations which beyond all question reduce our truly cultured nations to the barbarous standards of savage peoples.

IV.

VICES OPPOSED TO CHRISTIAN MARRIAGE

53. And now, Venerable Brethren, we shall explain in detail the evils opposed to each of the benefits of matrimony. First consideration is due to the offspring, which many have the boldness to call the disagreeable burden of matrimony, and which they say is to be carefully avoided by married people not through virtuous continence (which Christian law permits in matrimony when both parties consent) but by frustrating the marriage act. Some justify this criminal abuse on the ground that they are weary of children and wish to gratify their desires without their consequent burden. Others say that they cannot on the one hand remain continent, nor on the other can they have children, because of difficulties whether on the part of the mother or on the part of family circumstances.

54. But no reason, however grave, may be put forward by which anything intrinsically against nature may become conformable to nature and morally good. Since, therefore, the conjugal act is destined primarily by nature for the begetting of children, those who in exercising it deliberately frustrate its natural power and purpose, sin against nature and commit a deed which is shameful and intrinsically vicious.

55. Small wonder, therefore, if Holy Writ bears witness that the Divine Majesty regards with greatest detestation this

horrible crime and at times has punished it with death. As St. Augustine notes, "Intercourse even with one's legitimate wife is unlawful and wicked where the conception of the offspring is prevented. Onan, the son of Judah, did this and the Lord killed him for it."[27]

56. Since, therefore, openly departing from the uninterrupted Christian tradition, some recently have judged it possible solemnly to declare another doctrine regarding this question, the Catholic Church, to whom God has entrusted the defense of the integrity and purity of morals, standing erect in the midst of the moral ruin which surrounds her, in order that she may preserve the chastity of the nuptial union from being defiled by this foul stain, raises her voice in token of her divine ambassadorship and through Our mouth proclaims anew: any use whatsoever of matrimony exercised in such a way that the act is deliberately frustrated in its natural power to generate life is an offense against the law of God and of nature, and those who indulge in such are branded with the guilt of a grave sin.

57. We admonish, therefore, priests who hear confessions and others who have the care of souls, in virtue of Our supreme authority and in Our solicitude for the salvation of souls, not to allow the faithful entrusted to them to err regarding this most grave law of God; much more, that they keep themselves immune from such false opinions, in no way conniving in them. If any confessor or pastor of souls, who, may God forbid, lead the faithful entrusted to him into these errors or should at least confirm them by approval or by guilty

---

27. St. Augustine, *De coniug. adult.,* lib. II, n. 12, Gen 38:8–10.

silence, let him be mindful of the fact that he must render a strict account to God, the Supreme Judge, for the betrayal of his sacred trust, and let him take to himself the words of Christ: "They are blind and leaders of the blind, and if the blind lead the blind, both fall into the pit" (Mt 15:14).

58. As regards the evil use of matrimony, to pass over the arguments which are shameful, not infrequently others that are false and exaggerated are put forward. Holy Mother Church very well understands and clearly appreciates all that is said regarding the health of the mother and the danger to her life. And who would not grieve to think of these things? Who is not filled with the greatest admiration when he sees a mother risking her life with heroic fortitude, that she may preserve the life of the offspring which she has conceived? God alone, all bountiful and all merciful as he is, can reward her for the fulfillment of the office allotted to her by nature, and will assuredly repay her in a measure full to overflowing (Lk 6:38).

59. Holy Church knows well that not infrequently one of the parties is sinned against rather than sinning, when for a grave cause he or she reluctantly allows the perversion of the right order. In such a case, there is no sin, provided that, mindful of the law of charity, he or she does not neglect to seek to dissuade and to deter the partner from sin. Nor are those considered as acting against nature who in the married state use their right in the proper manner although on account of natural reasons either of time or of certain defects, new life cannot be brought forth. For in matrimony as well as in the use of the matrimonial rights there are also secondary ends, such as mutual aid, the cultivating of mutual love, and the

quieting of concupiscence, which husband and wife are not forbidden to consider so long as they are subordinated to the primary end and so long as the intrinsic nature of the act is preserved.

60. We are deeply touched by the sufferings of those parents who, in extreme want, experience great difficulty in rearing their children.

61. However, they should take care lest the calamitous state of their external affairs should be the occasion for a much more calamitous error. No difficulty can arise that justifies putting aside the law of God which forbids all acts intrinsically evil. There is no possible circumstance in which husband and wife cannot, strengthened by the grace of God, fulfill faithfully their duties and preserve in wedlock their chastity unspotted. This truth of Christian Faith is expressed by the teaching of the Council of Trent. "Let no one be so rash as to assert that which the Fathers of the Council have placed under anathema, namely, that there are precepts of God impossible for the just to observe. God does not ask the impossible, but by his commands, instructs you to do what you are able, to pray for what you are not able, that he may help you."[28]

62. This same doctrine was again solemnly repeated and confirmed by the Church in the condemnation of the Jansenist heresy which dared to utter this blasphemy against the goodness of God: "Some precepts of God are, when one considers the powers which man possesses, impossible of fulfillment

---

28. Council of Trent, Sess. 6, cap. 11.

even to the just who wish to keep the law and strive to do so; grace is lacking whereby these laws could be fulfilled."[29]

63. But another very grave crime is to be noted, Venerable Brethren, which regards the taking of the life of the offspring hidden in the mother's womb. Some wish it to be allowed and left to the will of the father or the mother; others say it is unlawful unless there are weighty reasons which they call by the name of medical, social or eugenic "indication." Because this matter falls under the penal laws of the state by which the destruction of the offspring begotten but unborn is forbidden, these people demand that the "indication," which in one form or another they defend, be recognized as such by the public law and in no way penalized. There are those, moreover, who ask that the public authorities provide aid for these death-dealing operations, a thing, which, sad to say, everyone knows is of very frequent occurrence in some places.

64. As to the "medical and therapeutic indication" to which, using their own words, we have made reference, Venerable Brethren, however much we may pity the mother whose health and even life is gravely imperiled in the performance of the duty allotted to her by nature, nevertheless, what could ever be a sufficient reason for excusing in any way the direct murder of the innocent? This is precisely what we are dealing with here. Whether inflicted upon the mother or upon the child, it is against the precept of God and the law of nature: "Thou shalt not kill."[30] The life of each is

---

29. Apostolic Constitution *Cum Occasione,* May 31, 1653, prop. 1.

30. Ex 20:13; cf. Decree of the Holy Office, May 4, 1897; July 24, 1895; May 31, 1884.

equally sacred, and no one, not even the public authority, has the power to destroy it. It is of no use to appeal to the right of taking away life, for here it is a question of the innocent, whereas that right has regard only to the guilty; nor is there here question of defense by bloodshed against an unjust aggressor (for who would call an innocent child an unjust aggressor?); again there is no question here of what is called the "law of extreme necessity" which could even extend to the direct killing of the innocent. Upright and skillful doctors strive most praiseworthily to guard and preserve the lives of both mother and child; on the contrary, those show themselves most unworthy of the noble medical profession who encompass the death of one or the other, through a pretense at practicing medicine or through motives of misguided pity.

65. All of which agrees with the stern words of the Bishop of Hippo in denouncing those wicked parents who seek to remain childless, and failing in this, are not ashamed to put their offspring to death: "Sometimes this lustful cruelty or cruel lust goes so far as to seek to procure a baneful sterility, and if this fails the fetus conceived in the womb is in one way or another smothered or evacuated, in the desire to destroy the offspring before it has life, or if it already lives in the womb, to kill it before it is born. If both man and woman are party to such practices they are not spouses at all; and if from the first they have carried on thus they have come together not for honest wedlock, but for impure gratification. If both are not party to these deeds, I make bold to say that either the one

makes herself a mistress of the husband, or the other simply the paramour of his wife."[31]

66. What is asserted in favor of the social and eugenic "indication" may and must be accepted, provided lawful and upright methods are employed within the proper limits. But to wish to put forward reasons based upon them for the killing of the innocent is unthinkable and contrary to the divine precept promulgated in the words of the Apostle: evil is not to be done that good may come of it (Rom 3:8).

67. Those who hold the reins of government should not forget that it is the duty of public authority by appropriate laws and sanctions to defend the lives of the innocent, and this all the more so since those whose lives are endangered and assailed cannot defend themselves. Among whom we must mention in the first place are infants hidden in the mother's womb. And if the public magistrates not only do not defend them, but by their laws and ordinances betray them to death at the hands of doctors or of others, let them remember that God is the Judge and Avenger of innocent blood which cried from earth to heaven (Gen 4:10).

Sterilization

68. Finally, that pernicious practice must be condemned which closely touches upon the natural right of man to enter matrimony, but affects also in a real way the welfare of the

---

31. St. Augustine, *De nupt. et concup.*, cap. XV.

offspring. For there are some who, over solicitous for the cause of eugenics, not only give salutary counsel for more certainly procuring the strength and health of the future child—which, indeed, is not contrary to right reason—but put eugenics before aims of a higher order, and by public authority wish to prevent from marrying all those whom, even though naturally fit for marriage, they consider, according to the norms and conjectures of their investigations, would, through hereditary transmission, bring forth defective offspring. And more, they wish to legislate to deprive these of that natural faculty by medical action despite their unwillingness; and this they do not propose as an infliction of grave punishment under the authority of the state for a crime committed, nor to prevent future crimes by guilty persons, but against every right and good they wish the civil authority to arrogate to itself a power over a faculty which it never had and can never legitimately possess.

69. Those who act in this way are at fault in losing sight of the fact that the family is more sacred than the State, and that men are begotten not for the earth and for time, but for heaven and eternity. Although often these individuals are to be dissuaded from entering into matrimony, certainly it is wrong to brand men with the stigma of crime because they contract marriage, on the ground that, despite the fact that they are in every respect capable of matrimony, they will give birth only to defective children, even though they use all care and diligence.

70. Public magistrates have no direct power over the bodies of their subjects; therefore, where no crime has taken place

and there is no cause present for grave punishment, they can never directly harm, or tamper with the integrity of the body, either for the reasons of eugenics or for any other reason. St. Thomas teaches this when, inquiring whether human judges for the sake of preventing future evils can inflict punishment, he admits that the power indeed exists as regards certain other forms of evil, but justly and properly denies it as regards the maiming of the body. "No one who is guiltless may be punished by a human tribunal either by flogging to death, or mutilation, or by beating."[32]

71. Furthermore, Christian doctrine establishes, and the light of human reason makes it most clear, that private individuals have no other power over the members of their bodies than that which pertains to their natural ends; and they are not free to destroy or mutilate their members, or in any other way render themselves unfit for their natural functions, except when no other provision can be made for the good of the whole body.

72. We may now consider another class of errors concerning conjugal faith. Every sin committed as regards the offspring becomes in some way a sin against conjugal faith, since both these blessings are essentially connected. However, we must mention briefly the sources of error and vice corresponding to those virtues which are demanded by conjugal faith, namely the chaste honor existing between man and wife, the due subjection of wife to husband, and the true love which binds both parties together.

---

32. *Summa Theol.*, 2a 2ae, q. 108, a. 4, ad 2.

"Thou Shalt Not Commit Adultery"

73. It follows, therefore, that they are destroying mutual fidelity who think that the ideas and morality of our present time concerning a certain harmful and false friendship with a third party can be countenanced, and who teach that a greater freedom of feeling and action in such external relations should be allowed to man and wife, particularly as many (so they consider) are possessed of an inborn sexual tendency which cannot be satisfied within the narrow limits of monogamous marriage. That rigid attitude which condemns all sensual affections and actions with a third party they imagine to be a narrowing of mind and heart, something obsolete, or an abject form of jealousy, and as a result they look upon whatever penal laws are passed by the State for preserving conjugal faith as void or to be abolished. Such unworthy and idle opinions are condemned by that noble instinct which is found in every chaste husband and wife, and even by the light of the testimony of nature alone—a testimony that is sanctioned and confirmed by the command of God: "Thou shalt not commit adultery" (Ex 20:14), and the words of Christ: "Whosoever shall look on a woman to lust after her has already committed adultery with her in his heart" (Mt 5:28). The force of this divine precept can never be weakened by any merely human custom, bad example or pretext of human progress, for just as it is the one and the same "Jesus Christ, yesterday and today and the same forever" (Heb 13:8), so it is the one and the same doctrine of Christ that abides and of which no one jot or tittle shall pass away till all is fulfilled (Mt 5:18).

74. The same false teachers who try to dim the luster of conjugal faith and purity do not scruple to do away with the

honorable and trusting obedience which the woman owes to the man. Many of them even go further and assert that such a subjection of one party to the other is unworthy of human dignity, that the rights of husband and wife are equal; wherefore, they boldly proclaim that the emancipation of women has been or ought to be effected. This emancipation, in their ideas, must be threefold, in the ruling of the domestic society, in the administration of family affairs and in the rearing of the children. It must be social, economic, physiological—physiological, that is to say, the woman is to be freed at her own good pleasure from the burdensome duties properly belonging to a wife as companion and mother (We have already said that this is not an emancipation but a crime); social, inasmuch as the wife being freed from the cares of children and family, should, to the neglect of these, be able to follow her own bent and devote herself to business and even public affairs; finally economic, whereby the woman even without the knowledge and against the wish of her husband may be at liberty to conduct and administer her own affairs, giving her attention chiefly to these rather than to children, husband and family.

75. This, however, is not the true emancipation of woman, nor that rational and exalted liberty which belongs to the noble office of a Christian woman and wife; it is rather the debasing of the womanly character and the dignity of motherhood, and indeed of the whole family, as a result of which the husband suffers the loss of his wife, the children of their mother, and the home and the whole family of an ever watchful guardian. More than this, this false liberty and unnatural equality with the husband is to the detriment of the woman herself, for if the woman descends from her truly regal throne

to which she has been raised within the walls of the home by means of the Gospel, she will soon be reduced to the old state of slavery (if not in appearance, certainly in reality) and become as among the pagans the mere instrument of man.

76. This equality of rights which is so much exaggerated and distorted, must indeed be recognized in those rights which belong to the dignity of the human soul and which are proper to the marriage contract and inseparably bound up with wedlock. In such things undoubtedly both parties enjoy the same rights and are bound by the same obligations; in other things there must be a certain inequality and due accommodation, which is demanded by the good of the family and the right ordering and unity and stability of home life.

77. As, however, the social and economic conditions of the married woman must in some way be altered on account of the changes in social intercourse, it is part of the office of the public authority to adapt the civil rights of the wife to modern needs and requirements, keeping in view what the natural disposition and temperament of the female sex, good morality, and the welfare of the family demands, and provided always that the essential order of the domestic society remain intact, founded as it is on something higher than human authority and wisdom, namely on the authority and wisdom of God, and so not changeable by public laws or at the pleasure of private individuals.

78. These enemies of marriage go further, however, when they substitute for that true and solid love, which is the basis of conjugal happiness, a certain vague compatibility of temperament. This they call sympathy and assert that, since it is the only bond by which husband and wife are linked together,

when it ceases the marriage is completely dissolved. What else is this than to build a house upon sand?—a house that in the words of Christ would forthwith be shaken and collapse, as soon as it was exposed to the waves of adversity: "And the winds blew and they beat upon that house. And it fell, and great was the fall thereof" (Mt 7:27). On the other hand, the house built upon a rock, that is to say on mutual conjugal chastity and strengthened by a deliberate and constant union of spirit, will not only never fall away but will never be shaken by adversity.

79. We have so far, Venerable Brethren, shown the excellence of the first two blessings of Christian wedlock, which the modern converters of society are attacking. And now considering that the third blessing, which is that of the sacrament, far surpasses the other two, we should not be surprised to find that this, because of its outstanding excellence, is much more sharply attacked by the same people. They put forward in the first place that matrimony belongs entirely to the profane and purely civil sphere, that it is not to be committed to the religious society, the Church of Christ, but to civil society alone. They then add that the marriage contract is to be freed from any indissoluble bond, and that separation and divorce are not only to be tolerated but sanctioned by the law; from which it follows finally that, robbed of all its holiness, matrimony should be enumerated among the secular and civil institutions. The first point is contained in their contention that the civil act itself should stand for the marriage contract (civil matrimony, as it is called), while the religious act is to be considered a mere addition, or at most a concession to a too superstitious people. Moreover they want it to be no cause for

reproach that marriages be contracted by Catholics with non-Catholics without any reference to religion or recourse to the ecclesiastical authorities. The second point which is but a consequence of the first is to be found in their excuse for complete divorce and in their praise and encouragement of those civil laws which favor the loosening of the bond itself. As the salient features of the religious character of all marriage, and particularly of the sacramental marriage of Christians, have been treated at length and supported by weighty arguments in the encyclical letters of Leo XIII, letters which We have frequently recalled to mind and expressly made our own, We refer you to them, repeating here only a few points.

Marriage Is a Sacrament

80. Even by the light of reason alone and particularly if the ancient records of history are investigated, if the unwavering popular conscience is interrogated and the manners and institutions of all races examined, it is sufficiently obvious that there is a certain sacredness and religious character attaching even to the purely natural union of man and woman, "not something added by chance but innate, not imposed by men but involved in the nature of things," since it has "God for its author and has been even from the beginning a foreshadowing of the Incarnation of the Word of God."[33] This sacredness of marriage, which is intimately connected with religion and all that is holy, arises from the divine origin we have just mentioned, from its purpose which is the begetting

---

33. Leo XIII, Encyclical *Arcanum,* Feb. 10, 1880.

and education of children for God, and the binding of man and wife to God through Christian love and mutual support; and finally it arises from the very nature of wedlock, whose institution is to be sought for in the farseeing Providence of God, whereby it is the means of transmitting life, thus making the parents the ministers, as it were, of the Divine Omnipotence. To this must be added that new element of dignity which comes from the sacrament, by which the Christian marriage is so ennobled and raised to such a level, that it appeared to the Apostle as a great sacrament, honorable in every way (Eph 5:32; Heb 13:4).

81. This religious character of marriage, its sublime signification of grace and the union between Christ and the Church, evidently requires that those about to marry should show a holy reverence toward it, and zealously endeavor to make their marriage approach as nearly as possible to the archetype of Christ and the Church.

Mixed Marriages

82. They, therefore, who rashly and heedlessly contract mixed marriages, from which the maternal love and providence of the Church dissuades her children for very sound reasons, fail conspicuously in this respect, sometimes with danger to their eternal salvation. This attitude of the Church to mixed marriages appears in many of her documents, all of which are summed up in the *Code of Canon Law:* "Everywhere and with the greatest strictness the Church forbids marriages between baptized persons, one of whom is a Catholic and the other a member of a schismatical or heretical sect;

and if there is, added to this, the danger of the falling away of the Catholic party and the perversion of the children, such a marriage is forbidden also by the divine law."[34] If the Church occasionally on account of circumstances does not refuse to grant a dispensation from these strict laws (provided that the divine law remains intact and the dangers mentioned above are provided against by suitable safeguards), it is unlikely that the Catholic party will not suffer some detriment from such a marriage.

83. Whence it comes about not infrequently, as experience shows, that deplorable defections from religion occur among the offspring, or at least a headlong descent into that religious indifference which is closely allied to impiety. There is this also to be considered, that in these mixed marriages it becomes much more difficult to imitate by a lively conformity of spirit the mystery of which We have spoken, namely that close union between Christ and his Church.

84. Assuredly, also, will there be wanting that close union of spirit which, as it is the sign and mark of the Church of Christ, so also should be the sign of Christian wedlock, its glory and adornment. For, where there exists diversity of mind, truth and feeling, the bond of union of mind and heart is wont to be broken, or at least weakened. From this comes the danger lest the love of man and wife grow cold and the peace and happiness of family life, resting as it does on the union of hearts, be destroyed. Many centuries ago indeed, the old Roman law had proclaimed: "Marriages are the union of male and female, a sharing of life and the communication of divine

---

34. *Code of Canon Law*, can. 1060.

and human rights."[35] But especially, as We have pointed out, Venerable Brethren, the daily increasing facility of divorce is an obstacle to the restoration of marriage to that state of perfection which the divine Redeemer willed it should possess.

Legalized Divorce

85. The advocates of the neopaganism of today have learned nothing from the sad state of affairs, but instead, day by day, more and more vehemently, they continue by legislation to attack the indissolubility of the marriage bond, proclaiming that the lawfulness of divorce must be recognized, and that the antiquated laws should give place to a new and more humane legislation. Many and varied are the grounds put forward for divorce, some arising from the wickedness and the guilt of the persons concerned, others arising from the circumstances of the case; the former they describe as subjective, the latter as objective; in a word, whatever might make married life hard or unpleasant. They strive to prove by various arguments their contentions regarding these grounds for the divorce legislation they would bring about. Thus, in the first place, they maintain that it is for the good of either party that the one who is innocent should have the right to separate from the guilty, or that the guilty should be withdrawn from a union which is unpleasing to him and against his will. In the second place, they argue, the good of the child demands this, for either it will be deprived of a proper education or the

---

35. Modestinus, *In Dig.* (Lib. 23, II: *De ritu nuptiarum*), lib. I, *Regularum.*

natural fruits of it, and will too easily be affected by the discords and shortcomings of the parents, and drawn from the path of virtue. And thirdly the common good of society requires that these marriages should be completely dissolved, which are now incapable of producing their natural results, and that legal reparations should be allowed when crimes are to be feared as the result of the common habitation and intercourse of the parties. This last, they say, must be admitted to avoid the crimes being committed purposely with a view to obtaining the desired sentence of divorce for which the judge can legally loose the marriage bond, as also to prevent people from coming before the courts when it is obvious from the state of the case that they are lying and perjuring themselves—all of which brings the court and the lawful authority into contempt. Hence the civil laws, in their opinion, have to be reformed to meet these new requirements, to suit the changes of the times and the changes in men's opinions, civil institutions and customs. Each of these reasons is considered by them as conclusive, so that all taken together offer a clear proof of the necessity of granting divorce in certain cases.

86. Others, taking a step further, simply state that marriage, being a private contract, is, like other private contracts, to be left to the consent and good pleasure of both parties, and so can be dissolved for any reason whatsoever.

God Forbids Divorce

87. Opposed to all these reckless opinions, Venerable Brethren, stands the unalterable law of God, fully confirmed by Christ, a law that can never be deprived of its force by the

decrees of men, the ideas of a people or the will of any legislator: "What God has joined together, let no man put asunder" (Mt 19:6). And if any man, acting contrary to this law, shall have put asunder, his action is null and void, and the consequence remains, as Christ himself has explicitly confirmed: "Everyone who puts away his wife and marries another, commits adultery, and he who marries her who is put away from her husband commits adultery" (Lk 16:18). Moreover, these words refer to every kind of marriage, even that which is natural and legitimate only; for, as has already been observed, that indissolubility by which the loosening of the bond is once and for all removed from the whim of the parties and from every secular power, is a property of every true marriage.

88. Let that solemn pronouncement of the Council of Trent be recalled to mind in which, under the stigma of anathema, it condemned these errors: "If anyone should say that on account of heresy or the hardships of cohabitation or a deliberate abuse of one party by the other the marriage tie may be loosened, let him be anathema;"[36] and again: "If anyone should say that the Church errs in having taught or in teaching that, according to the teaching of the Gospel and the Apostles, the bond of marriage cannot be loosed because of the sin of adultery of either party; or that neither party, even though he be innocent, having given no cause for the sin of adultery, can contract another marriage during the lifetime of the other; and that he commits adultery who marries another after putting away his adulterous wife, and likewise that she commits adul-

---

36. Council of Trent, Sess. 24, cap. 5.

tery who puts away her husband and marries another, let him be anathema."[37]

89. If therefore the Church has not erred and does not err in teaching this, and consequently it is certain that the bond of marriage cannot be loosed even on account of the sin of adultery, it is evident that all the other weaker excuses that can be and are usually brought forward, are of no value whatsoever. And the objections brought against the firmness of the marriage bond are easily answered. For, in certain circumstances, imperfect separation of the parties is allowed, the bond not being severed. This separation, which the Church herself permits, and expressly mentions in her canon law in those canons which deal with the separation of the parties as to marital relationship and cohabitation, removes all the alleged inconveniences and dangers.[38] It will be for the sacred law and, to some extent, also the civil law, insofar as civil matters are affected, to lay down the grounds, the conditions, the method and precautions to be taken in a case of this kind in order to safeguard the education of the children and the well-being of the family, and to remove all those evils which threaten the married persons, the children and the State. Now all those arguments that are brought forward to prove the indissolubility of the marriage tie, arguments which have already been touched upon, can equally be applied to excluding not only the necessity of divorce, but even the power to grant it; while for all the advantages that can be put forward for the former, there can be

---

37. Council of Trent, Sess. 24, cap. 7.
38. *Code of Canon Law*, can. 1128ff.

adduced as many disadvantages and evils which are a formidable menace to the whole of human society.

Evils of Divorce

90. To revert again to the expression of Our predecessor, it is hardly necessary to point out what an amount of good is involved in the absolute indissolubility of wedlock and what a train of evils follows upon divorce. Whenever the marriage bond remains intact, then we find marriages contracted with a sense of safety and security, while, when separations are considered and the dangers of divorce are present, the marriage contract itself becomes insecure, or at least gives ground for anxiety and surprises. On the one hand we see a wonderful strengthening of goodwill and cooperation in the daily life of husband and wife, while, on the other, both of these are miserably weakened by the presence of a facility for divorce. Here we have at a very opportune moment a source of help by which both parties are enabled to preserve their purity and loyalty; there we find harmful inducements to unfaithfulness. On this side we find the birth of children and their tuition* and upbringing effectively promoted, many avenues of discord closed among families and relations, and the beginnings of rivalry and jealousy easily suppressed; on that, very great obstacles to the birth and rearing of children and their education, and many occasions of quarrels, and seeds of jealousy sown everywhere. Finally, but especially, the dignity and position of women in civil and domestic society is reinstated by

---

* Older usage meaning guardianship or protection. *Ed.*

the former; while by the latter it is shamefully lowered and the danger is incurred "of their being considered outcasts, slaves of the lust of men."[39]

91. To conclude with the important words of Leo XIII, since the destruction of family life "and the loss of national wealth is brought about more by the corruption of morals than by anything else, it is easily seen that divorce, which is born of the perverted morals of a people, and leads, as experiment shows, to vicious habits in public and private life, is particularly opposed to the well-being of the family and of the State. The serious nature of these evils will be the more clearly recognized when we remember that, once divorce has been allowed, there will be no sufficient means of keeping it in check within any definite bounds. Great is the force of example, greater still that of lust; and with such incitements it cannot but happen that divorce and its consequent setting loose of the passions should spread daily and attack the souls of many like a contagious disease or a river bursting its banks and flooding the land."[40]

92. Thus, as we read in the same letter, "unless things change, the human family and State have every reason to fear lest they should suffer absolute ruin."[41] All this was written fifty years ago, yet it is confirmed by the daily increasing corruption of morals and the unheard of degradation of the family in those lands where Communism reigns unchecked.

---

39. Leo XIII, *Arcanum Divinae Sapientiae,* Feb. 10, 1880.

40. Encyclical *Arcanum Divinae Sapientiae,* Feb. 10, 1880.

41. Encyclical *Arcanum Divinae Sapientiae,* Feb. 10, 1880.

93. Thus far, Venerable Brethren, We have admired with due reverence what the all-wise Creator and Redeemer of the human race has ordained with regard to human marriage; at the same time we have expressed Our grief that such a pious ordinance of the divine Goodness should today, and on every side, be frustrated and trampled upon by the passions, errors and vices of men.

V.

REMEDIES

94. It is then fitting that, with all fatherly solicitude, We should turn Our mind to seek out suitable remedies whereby those most detestable abuses which We have mentioned may be removed, and everywhere marriage may again be revealed. To this end, it behooves Us, above all else, to call to mind that firmly established principle, esteemed alike in sound philosophy and sacred theology: namely, that whatever things have deviated from their right order, cannot he brought back to that original state which is in harmony with their nature except by a return to the divine plan which, as the Angelic Doctor teaches,[42] is the exemplar of all right order.

95. Wherefore, Our predecessor of happy memory, Leo XIII, attacked the doctrine of the naturalists in these words: "It is a divinely appointed law that whatsoever things are constituted by God, the Author of nature, these we find the more useful and salutary, the more they remain in their natural state, unimpaired and unchanged; inasmuch as God, the Creator of all things, intimately knows what is suited to the constitution and the preservation of each, and by his will and mind has so ordained all this that each may duly achieve its purpose. But if the boldness and wickedness of men change

---

42. St. Thomas Aquinas, *Summa Theol.,* Ia 2ae, q. 91, a. 1–2 .

and disturb this order of things, so providentially disposed, then, indeed, things so wonderfully ordained will begin to be injurious, or will cease to be beneficial, either because, in the change, they have lost their power to benefit, or because God himself is thus pleased to draw down chastisement on the pride and presumption of men."[43]

96. In order, therefore, to restore due order in this matter of marriage, it is necessary that all should bear in mind what is the divine plan and strive to conform to it.

Divinely Ordained Plan

97. Wherefore, since the chief obstacle to this study is the power of unbridled lust, which indeed is the most potent cause of sinning against the sacred laws of matrimony, and since man cannot hold in check his passions, unless he first subject himself to God, this must be his primary endeavor, in accordance with the plan divinely ordained. For it is a sacred ordinance that whoever shall have first subjected himself to God will, by the aid of divine grace, be glad to subject to himself his own passions and concupiscence; while he who is a rebel against God will, to his sorrow, experience within himself the violent rebellion of his worst passions.

98. And how wisely this has been decreed St. Augustine thus shows: "This indeed is fitting, that the lower be subject to the higher, so that he who would have subject to himself whatever is below him, should himself submit to whatever is above him. Acknowledge order, seek peace. Be subject to

---

43. Encyclical *Arcanum Divinae Sapientiae,* Feb. 10, 1880.

God, and your flesh subject to you. What more fitting! What more fair! You are subject to the higher and the lower is subject to you. Do you serve him who made you, so that that which was made for you may serve you. For we do not commend this order, namely, 'The flesh to you and you to God,' but 'You to God, and the flesh to you.' If, however, you despise the subjection of yourself to God, you shall never bring about the subjection of the flesh to yourself. If you do not obey the Lord, you shall be tormented by your servant."[44] This right ordering on the part of God's wisdom is mentioned by the holy Doctor of the Gentiles, inspired by the Holy Ghost, for in speaking of those ancient philosophers who refused to adore and reverence him whom they knew to be the Creator of the universe, he says: "Wherefore God gave them up to the desires of their heart, unto uncleanness, to dishonor their own bodies among themselves"; and again: "For this same God delivered them up to shameful affections" (Rom 1:24, 26). And St. James says: "God resists the proud and gives grace to the humble" (Jas 4:6), without which grace, as the same Doctor of the Gentiles reminds us, man cannot subdue the rebellion of his flesh (Rom 7:8).

99. Consequently, as the onslaughts of these uncontrolled passions cannot in any way be lessened, unless the spirit first shows a humble compliance of duty and reverence toward its Maker, it is above all and before all needful that those who are joined in the bond of sacred wedlock should be wholly imbued with a profound and genuine sense of duty toward God,

---

44. St. Augustine, *Enarrat. in Ps.,* 143.

which will shape their whole lives, and fill their minds and wills with a very deep reverence for the majesty of God.

100. Quite fittingly, therefore, and quite in accordance with the defined norm of Christian sentiment, do those pastors of souls act who, to prevent married people from failing in the observance of God's law, urge them to perform their duty and exercise their religion so that they should give themselves to God, continually ask for his divine assistance, frequent the sacraments, and always nourish and preserve a loyal and thoroughly sincere devotion to God.

101. They are greatly deceived who, having underestimated or neglected these means which rise above nature, think that they can induce men by the use and discovery of the natural sciences, such as those of biology, the science of heredity, and the like, to curb their carnal desires. We do not say this in order to belittle those natural means which are not dishonest; for God is the Author of nature as well as of grace, and he has disposed the good things of both orders for the beneficial use of men. The faithful, therefore, can and ought to be assisted also by natural means. But they are mistaken who think that these means are able to establish chastity in the nuptial union, or that they are more effective than supernatural grace.

102. This conformity of wedlock and moral conduct with the divine laws respective of marriage, without which its effective restoration cannot be brought about, supposes, however, that all can discern readily, with real certainty, and without any accompanying error, what those laws are. But everyone can see to how many fallacies an avenue would be opened up and how many errors would become mixed with

the truth, if it were left solely to the light of reason of each to find it out, or if it were to be discovered by the private interpretation of the truth which is revealed. And if this is applicable to many other truths of the moral order, we must all the more pay attention to those things which appertain to marriage where the inordinate desire for pleasure can attack frail human nature and easily deceive it and lead it astray; this is all the more true of the observance of the divine law, which demands sometimes hard and repeated sacrifices, for which, as experience points out, a weak man can find so many excuses for avoiding the fulfillment of the divine law.

103. On this account, in order that no falsification or corruption of the divine law but a true genuine knowledge of it may enlighten the minds of men and guide their conduct, it is necessary that a filial and humble obedience toward the Church should be combined with devotedness to God and the desire of submitting to him. For Christ himself made the Church the teacher of truth in those things also which concern the right regulation of moral conduct, even though some knowledge of the same is not beyond human reason. For just as God, in the case of the natural truths of religion and morals, added revelation to the light of reason so that what is right and true, "in the present state also of the human race may be known readily with real certainty without any admixture of error,"[45] so for the same purpose he has constituted the Church the guardian and the teacher of the whole of the truth concerning religion and moral conduct. To her, therefore, should the faithful show obedience and subject their minds and hearts so

---

45. First Vatican Council, Sess. 3, cap. 2.

as to be kept unharmed and free from error and moral corruption. And so that they shall not deprive themselves of that assistance given by God with such liberal bounty, they ought to show this due obedience not only when the Church defines something with solemn judgment, but also, in proper proportion, when by the constitutions and decrees of the Holy See, opinions are prescribed and condemned as dangerous or distorted.[46]

104. Wherefore, let the faithful also be on their guard against the overrated independence of private judgment and that false autonomy of human reason. For it is quite foreign to everyone bearing the name of a Christian to trust his own mental powers with such pride as to agree only with those things which he can examine from their inner nature, and to imagine that the Church, sent by God to teach and guide all nations, is not conversant with present affairs and circumstances; or even that they must obey only in those matters which she has decreed by solemn definition, as though her other decisions might be presumed to be false or putting forward insufficient motive for truth and honesty. Quite to the contrary, a characteristic of all true followers of Christ, lettered or unlettered, is to suffer themselves to be guided and led in all things that touch upon faith or morals by the Holy Church of God through its Supreme Pastor the Roman Pontiff, who is himself guided by Jesus Christ Our Lord.

---

46. First Vatican Council, Sess. 3, cap. 4; *Code of Canon Law,* can. 1324.

Complete Instruction

105. Consequently, since everything must be referred to the law and mind of God, in order to bring about the universal and permanent restoration of marriage, it is indeed of the utmost importance that the faithful should be well instructed concerning matrimony, both by word of mouth and by the written word, not cursorily but often and fully, by means of plain and weighty arguments, so that these truths will strike the intellect and will be deeply engraved on their hearts. Let them realize and diligently reflect upon the great wisdom, kindness and bounty God has shown toward the human race, not only by the institution of marriage, but also, and quite as much, by upholding it with sacred laws; still more, in wonderfully raising it to the dignity of a sacrament by which such an abundant fountain of graces has been opened to those joined in Christian wedlock, that these may be able to serve the noble purposes of wedlock for their own welfare and for that of their children, of the community and also for that of human relationship.

106. Certainly, if the latter day subverters of marriage are entirely devoted to misleading the minds of men and corrupting their hearts, to making a mockery of matrimonial purity and extolling the filthiest of vices by means of books and pamphlets and other innumerable methods, much more ought you, Venerable Brethren, whom "the Holy Ghost has placed as bishops, to rule the Church of God, which he has purchased with his own blood" (Acts 20:28), to give yourselves wholly to this, that through yourselves and through the priests subject to you, and, moreover, through the laity welded together by

Catholic Action, so much desired and recommended by Us, into a power of hierarchical apostolate, you may, by every fitting means, oppose error by truth, vice by the excellent dignity of chastity, the slavery of covetousness by the liberty of the sons of God (Jn 8:32 ff.; Gal 5:13), that disastrous ease in obtaining divorce by an enduring love in the bond of marriage, and by the inviolate pledge of fidelity given even to death.

107. Thus will it come to pass that the faithful will wholeheartedly thank God that they are bound together by his command and led by gentle compulsion to fly as far as possible from every kind of idolatry of the flesh and from the base slavery of the passions. They will, in a great measure, turn and be turned away from these abominable opinions which to the dishonor of man's dignity are now spread about in speech and in writing and collected under the title of "perfect marriage," and which indeed would make that perfect marriage nothing better than "depraved marriage," as it has been rightly and truly called.

108. Such wholesome instruction and religious training in regard to Christian marriage will be quite different from that exaggerated physiological education by means of which, in these times of ours, some reformers of married life make pretense of helping those joined in wedlock, laying much stress on these physiological matters, in which is learned rather the art of sinning in a subtle way than the virtue of living chastely.

109. So, Venerable Brethren, we make entirely Our own the words which Our predecessor of happy memory, Leo XIII, in his encyclical letter on Christian marriage addressed to the

bishops of the whole world: "Take care not to spare your efforts and authority in bringing about that among the people committed to your guidance that doctrine may be preserved whole and unadulterated which Christ the Lord and the apostles, the interpreters of the divine will, have handed down, and which the Catholic Church herself has religiously preserved, and commanded to be observed by the faithful of every age."[47]

Good Will to Obey

110. Even the very best instruction given by the Church, however, will not alone suffice to bring about once more conformity of marriage to the law of God; something more is needed in addition to the education of the mind, namely a steadfast determination of the will, on the part of husband and wife, to observe the sacred laws of God and of nature in regard to marriage. In fine, in spite of what others may wish to assert and spread abroad by word of mouth or in writing, let husband and wife resolve: to stand fast to the commandments of God in all things that matrimony demands; always to render to each other the assistance of mutual love; to preserve the honor of chastity; not to lay profane hands on the stable nature of the bond; to use the rights given them by marriage in a way that will be always Christian and sacred, more especially in the first years of wedlock, so that should there be need of continency afterward, custom will have made it easier for each to preserve it. In order that they may make this firm

---

47. Encyclical *Arcanum Divinae Sapientiae,* Feb. 10, 1880.

resolution, keep it and put it into practice, an oft-repeated consideration of their state of life, and a diligent reflection on the sacrament they have received, will be of great assistance to them. Let them constantly keep in mind that they have been sanctified and strengthened for the duties and for the dignity of their state by a special sacrament, the efficacious power of which, although it does not impress a character, is undying. To this purpose we may ponder the words full of real comfort of holy Cardinal Robert Bellarmine, who with other well-known theologians with devout conviction thus expresses himself: "The sacrament of Matrimony can be regarded in two ways: first, in the making, and then in its permanent state. For it is a sacrament like to that of the Eucharist, which not only when it is being conferred, but also while it remains, is a sacrament; for as long as the married parties are alive, so long is their union a sacrament of Christ and the Church."[48]

111. Yet in order that the grace of this sacrament may produce its full fruit, there is need, as we have already pointed out, for the cooperation of the married parties; which consists in their striving to fulfill their duties to the best of their ability and with unwearied effort. For just as in the natural order men must apply the powers given them by God with their own toil and diligence that these may exercise their full vigor, failing which, no profit is gained, so also men must diligently and unceasingly use the powers given them by the grace which is laid up in the soul by this sacrament. Let not, then, those who are joined in matrimony neglect the grace of the sacrament

---

48. St. Robert Bellarmine, *De controversiis,* tom. III, *De Matr.,* controvers. II, cap. 6.

which is in them (1 Tim 4:14); for, in applying themselves to the careful observance, however laborious, of their duties they will find the power of that grace becoming more effectual as time goes on. And if ever they should feel themselves to be overburdened by the hardships of their condition of life, let them not lose courage, but rather let them regard in some measure as addressed to them that which St. Paul the Apostle wrote to his beloved disciple Timothy regarding the sacrament of Holy Orders when the disciple was dejected through hardship and insults: "I admonish you to stir up the grace which is in you by the imposition of my hands. For God has not given us the spirit of fear; but of power and of love and of sobriety" (2 Tim 1:6–7).

Preparation for Marriage Needed

112. All these things, however, Venerable Brethren, depend in large measure on the due preparation, remote and proximate, of the parties for marriage. For it cannot be denied that the basis of a happy wedlock, and the ruin of an unhappy one, is prepared and set in the souls of boys and girls during the period of childhood and adolescence. There is danger that those who before marriage sought in all things what is theirs, who indulged even their impure desires, will be in the married state what they were before, that they will reap that which they have sown (Gal 6:9); indeed, within the home there will be sadness, lamentation, mutual contempt, strifes, estrangements, weariness of common life, and, worst of all, such parties will find themselves left alone with their own unconquered passions.

113. Let then those who are about to enter married life approach that state well disposed and well prepared, so that they will be able, as far as they can, to help each other in sustaining the vicissitudes of life, and yet more in attending to their eternal salvation and in forming the inner man unto the fullness of the age of Christ (Eph 4:13). It will also help them if they behave toward their cherished offspring as God wills: that is, that the father be truly a father, and the mother truly a mother; through their devout love and unwearying care, the home, though it suffer the want and hardship of this valley of tears, may become for the children in its own way a foretaste of that paradise of delight in which the Creator placed the first men of the human race. Thus will they be able to bring up their children as perfect men and perfect Christians; they will instill into them a sound understanding of the Catholic Church, and will give them such a disposition and love for their fatherland as duty and gratitude demand.

114. Consequently, both those who are now thinking of entering upon this sacred married state, as well as those who have the charge of educating Christian youth, should, with due regard to the future, prepare that which is good, obviate that which is bad, and recall those points about which We have already spoken in Our encyclical letter concerning education: "The inclinations of the will, if they are bad, must be repressed from childhood, but such as are good must be fostered, and the mind, particularly of children, should be imbued with doctrines which begin with God, while the heart should be strengthened with the aids of divine grace, in the absence of which no one can curb evil desires, nor can his discipline and formation be brought to complete perfection by

the Church. For Christ has provided her with heavenly doctrines and divine sacraments, that he might make her an effectual teacher of men."[49]

Choosing a Partner

115. To the proximate preparation of a good married life belongs very specially the care in choosing a partner; on that depends a great deal whether the forthcoming marriage will be happy or not, since one may be to the other either a great help in leading a Christian life, or a great danger and hindrance. And so that they may not deplore for the rest of their lives the sorrows arising from an indiscreet marriage, those about to enter into wedlock should carefully deliberate in choosing the person with whom henceforward they must live continually. They should, in so deliberating, keep before their minds the thought first of God and of the true religion of Christ, then of themselves, of their partner, of the children to come, as also of human and civil society, for which wedlock is a fountain head. Let them diligently pray for divine help, so that they make their choice in accordance with Christian prudence, not indeed led by the blind and unrestrained impulse of lust, nor by any desire of riches or other base influence, but by a true and noble love and by a sincere affection for the future partner, and then let them strive in their married life for those ends for which the state was constituted by God. Lastly, let them not omit to ask the prudent advice of their parents with regard to the partner, and let them regard this advice in no

---

49. Encyclical *Divini Illius Magistri,* Dec. 31, 1929.

light manner, in order that by their mature knowledge and experience of human affairs, they may guard against a disastrous choice, and, on the threshold of matrimony, may receive more abundantly the divine blessing of the fourth commandment: "Honor your father and your mother (which is the first commandment with a promise) that it may be well with you and you may be long-lived upon the earth" (Eph 6:2–3; Ex 20:12).

116. Now since it is no rare thing to find that the perfect observance of God's commands and conjugal integrity encounter difficulties by reason of the fact that the man and wife are in straitened circumstances, their necessities must be relieved as far as possible.

Necessary Economic Security

117. And so, in the first place, every effort must be made to bring about that which Our predecessor Leo XIII, of happy memory, has already insisted upon,[50] namely, that in the State such economic and social methods should be adopted as will enable every head of a family to earn as much as, according to his station in life, is necessary for himself, his wife, and for the rearing of his children, for "the laborer is worthy of his hire" (Lk 10:7). To deny this, or to make light of what is equitable, is a grave injustice and is placed among the greatest sins by Holy Writ (Dt 24:14–15); nor is it lawful to fix such a

---

50. Encyclical *Rerum Novarum,* May 15, 1891.

scanty wage as will be insufficient for the upkeep of the family in the circumstances in which it is placed.

118. Care, however, must be taken that the parties themselves, for a considerable time before entering upon married life, should strive to dispose of, or at least to diminish, the material obstacles in their way. The manner in which this may be done effectively and honestly must be pointed out by those who are experienced. Provision must be made also, in the case of those who are not self-supporting, for joint aid by private or public guilds.[51]

119. When these means which We have pointed out do not fulfill the needs, particularly of a larger or poorer family, Christian charity toward our neighbor absolutely demands that those things which are lacking to the needy should be provided; hence it is incumbent on the rich to help the poor, so that, having an abundance of this world's goods, they may not expend them fruitlessly or completely squander them, but employ them for the support and well-being of those who lack the necessities of life. They who give of their substance to Christ in the person of his poor will receive from the Lord a most bountiful reward when he shall come to judge the world; they who act to the contrary will pay the penalty (Mt 25:34 ff.). Not in vain does the Apostle warn us: "He who has the substance of this world and shall see his brother in need, and shall shut up his heart from him: how does the charity of God abide in him?" (1 Jn 3:17).

---

51. Leo XIII, Encyclical *Rerum Novarum,* May 15, 1891.

Obligation of the State

120. If, however, for this purpose private resources do not suffice, it is the duty of the public authority to supply for the insufficient forces of individual effort, particularly in a matter which is of such importance to the common weal, touching as it does the maintenance of the family and married people. If families, particularly those in which there are many children, have not suitable dwellings; if the husband cannot find employment and means of livelihood; if the necessities of life cannot be purchased except at exorbitant prices; if even the mother of the family, to the great harm of the home, is compelled to go forth and seek a living by her own labor; if she, too, in the ordinary or even extraordinary labors of childbirth, is deprived of proper food, medicine and the assistance of a skilled physician, it is patent to all to what an extent married people may lose heart, and how home life and the observance of God's commands are rendered difficult for them; indeed it is obvious how great a peril can arise to the public security and to the welfare and very life of civil society itself when such men are reduced to that condition of desperation that, having nothing which they fear to lose, they are emboldened to hope for chance advantage from the upheaval of the state and of established order.

121. Wherefore, those who have the care of the State and of the public good cannot neglect the needs of married people and their families, without bringing great harm upon the State and on the common welfare. Hence, in making the laws and in disposing of public funds they must do their utmost to relieve

the needs of the poor, considering such a task as one of the most important of their administrative duties.

122. We are sorry to note that not infrequently nowadays it happens that through a certain inversion of the true order of things, ready and bountiful assistance is provided for the unmarried mother and her illegitimate offspring (who, of course must be helped in order to avoid a greater evil) which is denied to legitimate mothers or given sparingly or almost grudgingly.

Authority of the Church

123. But not only in regard to temporal goods, Venerable Brethren, is it the concern of the public authority to make proper provision for matrimony and the family, but also in other things which concern the good of souls. Just laws must be made for the protection of chastity, for reciprocal conjugal aid, and for similar purposes, and these must be faithfully enforced, because, as history testifies, the prosperity of the State and the temporal happiness of its citizens cannot remain safe and sound where the foundation on which they are established, which is the moral order, is weakened, and where the very fountainhead from which the State draws its life, namely, wedlock and the family, is obstructed by the vices of its citizens.

124. For the preservation of the moral order neither the laws and sanctions of the temporal power are sufficient, nor is the beauty of virtue and the expounding of its necessity. Reli-

gious authority must enter in to enlighten the mind, to direct the will, and to strengthen human frailty by the assistance of divine grace. Such an authority is found nowhere save in the Church instituted by Christ the Lord. Hence We earnestly exhort in the Lord all those who hold the reins of power that they establish and maintain firmly harmony and friendship with this Church of Christ, so that through the united activity and energy of both powers the tremendous evils, fruits of those wanton liberties which assail both marriage and the family and are a menace to both Church and State, may be effectively frustrated.

The State and the Church

125. Governments can assist the Church greatly in the execution of its important office, if, in laying down their ordinances, they take account of what is prescribed by divine and ecclesiastical law, and if penalties are fixed for offenders. For as it is, there are those who think that whatever is permitted by the laws of the State, or at least is not punished by them, is allowed also in the moral order, and, because they neither fear God nor see any reason to fear the laws of man, they act even against their conscience, thus often bringing ruin upon themselves and upon many others. There will be no peril to or lessening of the rights and integrity of the State from its association with the Church. Such suspicion and fear is empty and groundless, as Leo XIII has already so clearly set forth: "It is generally agreed," he says, "that the Founder of the Church, Jesus Christ, wished the spiritual power to be distinct from the civil, and each to be free and unhampered in

doing its own work, not forgetting, however, that it is expedient to both, and in the interest of everybody, that there be a harmonious relationship.... If the civil power combines in a friendly manner with the spiritual power of the Church, it necessarily follows that both parties will greatly benefit. The dignity of the State will be enhanced, and with religion as its guide, there will never be a rule that is not just; while for the Church there will be at hand a safeguard and defense which will operate to the public good of the faithful."[52]

126. To bring forward a recent and clear example of what is meant, it has happened quite in consonance with right order and entirely according to the law of Christ, that in the solemn Convention happily entered into between the Holy See and the Kingdom of Italy, also in matrimonial affairs a peaceful settlement and friendly cooperation has been obtained, such as befitted the glorious history of the Italian people and its ancient and sacred traditions. These decrees are to be found in the Lateran Pact: "The Italian State, desirous of restoring to the institution of matrimony, which is the basis of the family, that dignity conformable to the traditions of its people, assigns as civil effects of the sacrament of Matrimony all that is attributed to it in canon law."[53] To this fundamental norm are added further clauses in the common pact.

127. This might well be a striking example to all of how, even in this our own day (in which, sad to say, the absolute separation of the civil power from the Church, and indeed from every religion, is so often taught), the one supreme

52. Encyclical *Arcanum Divinae Sapientiae,* Feb. 10, 1880.
53. Concord., art. 34; *AAS,* XXI (1929), p. 290.

authority can be united and associated with the other without detriment to the rights and supreme power of either, thus protecting Christian parents from pernicious evils and menacing ruin.

128. All these things which, Venerable Brethren, prompted by Our past solicitude We put before you, We wish according to the norm of Christian prudence to be promulgated widely among all Our beloved children committed to your care as members of the great family of Christ, that all may be thoroughly acquainted with sound teaching concerning marriage, so that they may be ever on their guard against the dangers advocated by the teachers of error, and most of all, that "denying ungodliness and worldly desires, they may live soberly and justly, and godly in this world, looking for the blessed hope and coming of the glory of the great God and Our Savior Jesus Christ" (Ti 2:12–13).

129. May the Father, "of whom all paternity in heaven and earth is named" (Eph 3:15), Who strengthens the weak and gives courage to the pusillanimous and fainthearted, and Christ Our Lord and Redeemer, "the Institutor and Perfecter of the holy sacraments,"[54] Who desired marriage to be and made it the mystical image of his own ineffable union with the Church; and the Holy Ghost, Love of God, the Light of hearts and the Strength of the mind, grant that all will perceive, will admit with a ready will, and by the grace of God will put into practice what We by this letter have expounded concerning the holy sacrament of Matrimony, the wonderful law and will of God respecting it, the errors and impending

---

54. Council of Trent, Sess. 24.

dangers, and the remedies with which they can be counter-acted, so that that fruitfulness dedicated to God will flourish again vigorously in Christian wedlock.

130. We most humbly pour forth Our earnest prayer at the Throne of his Grace, that God, the Author of all graces, the inspirer of all good desires and deeds (Phil 2:13), may bring this about, and deign to give it bountifully according to the greatness of his liberality and omnipotence, and as a token of the abundant blessing of the same Omnipotent God, We most lovingly grant to you, Venerable Brethren, and to the clergy and people committed to your watchful care, the apostolic benediction.

Given at Rome, in St. Peter's, this 31st day of December, of the year 1930, the ninth of Our pontificate.

Pius PP. XI.

Pauline
BOOKS & MEDIA

The Daughters of St. Paul operate book and media centers at the following addresses. Visit, call or write the one nearest you today, or find us on the World Wide Web, www.pauline.org

California
3908 Sepulveda Blvd, Culver City,
  CA 90230   310-397-8676
5945 Balboa Avenue, San Diego,
  CA 92111   858-565-9181
46 Geary Street, San Francisco,
  CA 94108   415-781-5180

Florida
145 S.W. 107th Avenue, Miami,
  FL 33174   305-559-6715

Hawaii
1143 Bishop Street, Honolulu, HI
  96813   808-521-2731

Neighbor Islands call: 800-259-8463

Illinois
172 North Michigan Avenue, Chicago,
  IL 60601   312-346-4228

Louisiana
4403 Veterans Memorial Blvd,
  Metairie, LA 70006   504-887-7631

Massachusetts
Rte. 1, 885 Providence Hwy,
  Dedham, MA 02026
  781-326-5385

Missouri
9804 Watson Road, St. Louis,
  MO 63126   314-965-3512

New Jersey
561 U.S. Route 1, Wick Plaza,
  Edison, NJ 08817
  732-572-1200

New York
150 East 52nd Street,
  New York, NY 10022
  212-754-1110
78 Fort Place, Staten Island, NY
  10301   718-447-5071

Ohio
2105 Ontario Street, Cleveland,
  OH 44115   216-621-9427

Pennsylvania
9171-A Roosevelt Blvd,
  Philadelphia, PA 19114
  215-676-9494

South Carolina
243 King Street, Charleston, SC
  29401   843-577-0175

Tennessee
4811 Poplar Avenue, Memphis,
  TN 38117   901-761-2987

Texas
114 Main Plaza, San Antonio, TX
  78205   210-224-8101

Virginia
1025 King Street, Alexandria, VA
  22314   703-549-3806

Canada
3022 Dufferin Street, Toronto,
  Ontario, Canada M6B 3T5
  416-781-9131
1155 Yonge Street, Toronto, Ontario,
  Canada M4T 1W2   416-934-3440

¡También somos su fuente para libros, videos y música en español!